FROM CRADLE TO BRAVE

MARIA B. HAYDEN

FROM CRADLE TO BRAVE

First published in 2020 in the United Kingdom
by Rebus Imprint

www.mariabhayden.com

introduction

this is my story
these are my memories
I'm sorry
I can't make it pretty
but read till the end
to discover
there is
freedom after abuse

contents

part one

1.

the mother screamed
for her life
her watching daughters
joined in
a battle from hell broke loose
that only the father could win

2.

oh, sweet lovely stranger
she dares not tell
that she is a child
living through hell
I know you can see
the pain in her eyes
but secrets are safety
that's how she survives

3.

the mother trusted the friend
with children of his own
that he would damage her
daughter
how could she ever have known

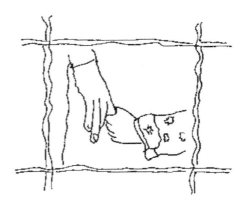

4.

dance pretty girl
let the music play
wiggle your hips
and let them sway
I know you trust me
I'm mummy's friend
let us share a moment
without an end
just come over here
and sit on my lap
let me introduce
the paedophiles' trap

5.

cold white walls
and a sterile bed
her mother replaced
with strangers instead
her sisters small hand
gripped into her own
so very grateful
she wasn't alone
guarded smiles
and a comforting word
the promise of safety
is what she heard
as sisters they merged
their future unknown
another lost cause
in a children's home
they cried for their mother
each single day
till their father came
to take them away

6.

dear Cinderella, we've met her
your stepmother's evil twin
only ours enjoys the beating
and sneers at our suffering
our father has chosen a silence
his daughters her unwilling prey
each day he heads out to work
she starves us and locks us away
we can't find the friendly mice
our godmother's lost her way
we pray that our mother returns
and live by our wits each day

7.

'smile for the camera my dear'
the news reporter said
*'you and your sister are very
brave, everyone feared you
were dead'*

8.

there was a bitter sweetness
in the baby that always cries
she arrived when we were lost
our sister with father's eyes

9.

you hand me a plastic doll
the image of what I should be
beautiful hair and a pretty face
she bears no resemblance to me
I stare at her big blue eyes
mine are a dirty brown
her locks are a shining gold
and she wears them like a crown
you tell me to play with her
that she is a gift from you
I smile and thank you at once
and hope that's
what daughters do

10.

the daughter straightened her back
her instincts making her stare
the mother giggled and smiled
at the man with the auburn hair
the noisy bar fell into silence
her eyes refused to budge
until her sister made her jump
by giving her a nudge
but the daughter couldn't help it
she knew that he was a stranger
had her mother lost her mind
and forgotten all the danger
as if the man could sense
the daughter's panic rise
he finally turned and smiled
with kindness in his eyes

11.

the daughter loved the sound
of her beautiful new surname
protected at last with disguise
from a past engulfed in shame

12.

a twisted magnetic pull resides
the hunter knows where the
victim hides
bullies get high on a
twisted game
use poisonous words of
hate and blame
the daughter is chased
around the school
this is the place where the
gangsters rule

13.

her sister cries
and breaks her heart
as only one suitcase
tears them apart
a new safe place
with trinkets and dust
the grandparents' home
shelters love and trust

14.

sweet boy you say
that you love me
I wish I believed
it was true
but the girl that you see
on the outside
is not the right
sweetheart for you
I am damaged by secrets I keep
ones that I'll take to my grave
I don't believe in a
knight on a horse
and I'm not a damsel to save

15.

the girl will turn into a woman
neither victim nor fighter yet
she will spend each day in her head
with a past she begs to forget

part two

16.

the fate of the fatherless
daughter
as she steps through the door
to leave home
is to search with an ache in
her heart
for a love that she can call her
own

17.

the hotel loomed up ahead
her world in a bag at her feet
wiser than words at sixteen
the future was hers to defeat
she trembled with nerves inside
and silenced the fear in her head
the gruelling job of a chambermaid
offered her food and a bed

18.

'you're so very pretty', he said
'there's a place for you in my
bed'
the fact that he wore a ring
didn't seem to mean a thing
he hounded me down for weeks
perfecting his chatter with
tweaks
each time that he came too near
I was frozen and rigid with fear
I hated the hierarchy
he was already on top of me
but he met the girl from the dirt
when he stuck his hand up my
skirt

19.

I cherished the boyfriend in tow
but the onlookers did not know
that he beat me with words
regularly
and I thought he was better than
me
in times when his words weren't
enough
then my back would hit the wall
one hand gripped 'round my
throat
and the other clenched into a ball

20.

do you know what you do
when you strike me again
you convince me
I'm worthless
and hated by men

21.

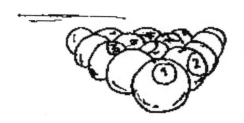

the gossiping girls at the bar
watch me with pitying eyes
I cuddle the arm of my boyfriend
and haven't a clue that he lies
the girls take their chance when
he leaves
to play a quick game of pool
and tell me that he is cheating
and treating me like a fool

22.

smile it might never happen
men that are strangers have said
but how can I sweetly smile
when my trust in them is dead

23.

come on, he said
I'll take you home
it's not safe for you
to travel alone
he seemed okay
the same age as me
and wasn't a stranger
how bad could it be
I have an idea
let's have coffee at mine
I think it's a shame
to end a good time
I walked like a lamb
straight into the slaughter
and forgot all I learnt
when I was the daughter

24.

the counsellor respected her wishes
the daughter would rather not say
if she keeps reliving the details
the horror won't go away
it's bad enough that it haunts her
her body is no longer her own
it bleeds as a constant reminder
she really should have gone home

25.

it can take years for justice
she wishes the bastard was dead
the policewoman guides her well
to move on with her life instead
she cannot face the trial
to prove she's not a whore
instead she takes
some sleeping pills
and ends up on the floor

26.

the road to healing is hard
there is no instant cure
but with her loving friends
she managed to endure
it also healed her mind
to know that he did not win
if she got on with her life
and grew stronger from within

27.

her world fell apart once more
the day that her grandfather died
her grandmother lost her mind
and something died inside

part three

28.

she wears her scars as an armour
as they do not belong in her heart
she has risen from out of the dirt
and longs for a brand-new start

29.

in the pretty new dress
as a bride to be
her body is rigid
with uncertainty
she craves all the safety
that marriage provides
so smiles through the fear
that she hides
the photographer clicked
when it is done
at the beautiful bride in the sun
the sisters look on from the side
their eyes shedding
tears of pride
the outer success of a life
hid the truth of the trophy wife

30.

the naive wife didn't choose well
the husband had put her
through hell
he liked to remind her that it
was *'he'*
who saved her from living in
poverty
and if he stepped back through
history
it wasn't his wife she would be
that noblemen claim it defeat
to marry a girl from the street

31.

it was three times
she lost a child
then something snapped -
something wild
when the husband
refused to accept
her grief as she sat and wept
she packed up all of her things
and left with only her rings

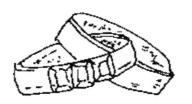

32.

the schoolboy sweetheart
swept into her life
so happy that she was
no longer a wife

33.

the daughter was no
longer wife
nor mother
as she had prayed
the sweetheart
found a new lover
and there he finally stayed

part four

34.

she held the keys in her hand
all alone at her own front
door
many steps had led her here
where freedom was hers to
explore

35.

as she stepped into her new life
and found her place on earth
loving the freedom of choices
she discovered her true self-worth

36.

like a spring flower
she rose from her grave
with hope in her heart
from broken to brave

37.

when you are
no longer looking
for a man
to take his place
the universe
finally sends him
and your soul
recognises his face

38.

he listened to every story
about the daughter's life
gently wiped the tears away
until she became his wife
together they fought the
challenge
of her infertility
until a special day arrived
to complete their family

39.

the husband's eyes met her own
as he carefully put down the phone
then came and sat at her feet
his shoulders hung in defeat
he softly shook his head
and whispered
your sister's dead
then gently told his wife
her sister had taken her life
she screamed until
silence came
just one little word
- her name

words for healing

40.

when we are truly vulnerable
we discover the greatest gift of all
that we all have a strength within
and there is only one way to win
to fight for your place on this earth
you begin by accepting your worth

41.

unchain yourself from the past
and believe the world
can be kind
you deserve
the best of everything
accept this to heal your mind

42.

you are the hero
in your own life story
grab your cloak
and head for glory

43.

we all search for love
and a deeper connection
taking separate roads
in the same direction

44.

our beliefs are what
hold us back
compounded by those
we meet
so carefully sift through
them all
and discard
the ones of defeat

45.

you were born
to this world unique
there is no other
version of you
remove all doubt
from your mind
there is nothing
you cannot do

46.

embrace your
warrior within
rise up - let the
battle begin

47.

this life is
a
series of
moments

48.

if you believe that you will fail
before you even try
then you have quit
before you start
and waved success goodbye

49.

a warrior lives within
the beating heart of
every woman

50.

you're one of a kind
in design
so hold up your head
and shine

51.

never let anyone
challenge your worth
you are a Goddess
that roams the Earth

52.

you are perfect
the way that you are
a unique and
beautiful star

53.

emotions are words
without a voice

54.

tears are how
the soul can weep
releasing the pain
it cannot keep

55.

in a world full of fear
with a storm up ahead
let hope be the
rainbow
that guides you instead

56.

before you decide
that you cannot cope
if you are still
breathing
then there is hope

57.

treasure those friends
who always try
to hold you steady
until you fly

58.

at times we all need
some perspective
and the best way to
cope with pain
is to pack your bags -
take some time out
until you feel stronger
again

59.

the only way to know
for sure
is reach for the handle
and open that door

60.

a broken woman
who finds her voice
will tell all the others
that they have a choice

61.

if you're staring down at the floor
and wondering what it's all for
let my words
gently lift your head
you are broken
but you are not dead
whatever has caused you pain
must not come to pass again
do not let this moment win
call your warrior hidden within
she will spring into action with ease
you do not belong on your knees
and though you may think I am wrong
you'll survive this because you are
strong

62.

be kind to yourself
healing takes time
you are a survivor
and victim of crime
millions of women
will tell you this too
one step at a time
will get you through

63.

justice is
served
by
your
survival

the end

dedicated to my sister Natalie

I would not have chosen to walk a single moment of this life without you as my sister. Part one was our story and testament to the loving bond that we share. When I look back it's almost unbelievable that we made it out alive but I think it's 100% down to that love. Still to this day – there isn't a thing I wouldn't do for you, even if it gets me into trouble.

this book is in loving memory of our baby sister *Abigail Sarah Jane*

Gone too soon

a letter for heaven

Dear Abigail,

I know it's too late, but I wish I had been brave for you sooner. I wish with all my heart that I had been able to encourage you to fight, and empower you with my love, compassion, and strength. You were wrong, the world is not better off without you. There were three of us in this together and now we are inexplicably incomplete. We light a candle for you every birthday, Christmas and on the day that you died, in the hope that you can see our love still burning for you in heaven.

I know you would want me to write this book to give others courage, but I'm also writing it for you, so that your precious life wasn't lost in vain.

Until we meet again,
all our love
Your sisters,
Maria & Natalie xxx

PLEASE LEAVE
A REVIEW FOR THIS BOOK
TO HELP OTHERS
FIND IT

If you like my work
and I hope that you do,
please help me find readers
and leave a review.
It won't take a moment
but let's others see,
there's room in their heart
for a writer like me.

*Reviews are so important for us authors
because they genuinely help other readers
find our books and they also let me know
that you liked it. Thank you.*

OTHER BOOKS BY MARIA B. HAYDEN

POETRY

POEMS ABOUT LOVE
POEMS ABOUT DARK TIMES
POEMS ABOUT LIFE
TO BE A WOMAN

CHILDREN'S

THE FAIRY SECRET
THE MERMAID WISH
WHICH WITCH AM I

SPECIAL OFFER FOR READERS OF THIS BOOK

Would you like one of Maria's poetry books for FREE?

She is giving away a **FREE DOWNLOAD** of **TO BE A WOMAN** for a **LIMITED TIME (Exclusive on her website)**

Lots more Goddess power and it's absolutely FREE. Go to the website and click 'claim my free book'.

www.mariabhayden.com